TIME GENTLEMEN

Also by Hamish Brown (in print)

THE ISLAND OF RHUM
HAMISH'S MOUNTAIN WALK
HAMISH'S GROATS END WALK
EYE TO THE HILLS (poems)
Edited: POEMS OF THE SCOTTISH HILLS
  an Anthology

Other AUP Poetry Titles

FOR ALL I KNOW *Ken Morrice*
THE PURE ACCOUNT poems by Olive Fraser
  ed. Helena M. Shire
THE DANCE IN THE VILLAGE AND OTHER
  POEMS *Christina Forbes Middleton*
ECHO OF MANY VOICES *Lilianne Grant Rich*
POEMS OF THE SCOTTISH HILLS   an Anthology
  ed. Hamish Brown

TIME GENTLEMEN

Some Collected Poems

HAMISH BROWN

Illustrations by Ian Strachan

ABERDEEN UNIVERSITY PRESS

First published 1983
Aberdeen University Press
A member of the Pergamon Group

The publisher acknowledges subsidy from the Scottish Arts Council towards the publication of this volume.

British Library Cataloguing in Publication Data

Brown, Hamish M.
  Time Gentlemen: some collected poems
  1. Title
  821'.914   PR6052. R/

  ISBN 0—08—030375—7

PRINTED IN GREAT BRITAIN
THE UNIVERSITY PRESS
ABERDEEN

FOR CHRISTINE AND JAMIE

Just a year since Donald died,
since the Allt na Ciche swept him away
into the loch? He was so impatient
with life, wanting to live a century in one burst —
a crazy athlete competing in every race.

A lonely rowan grows below the slope
where his ashes lie. He would like that
nameless memorial which speaks only to those
who knew him in the rush of days
and shared his hard, mountain attitudes
to life. At the New Year we remember; smile
for Donald, already on the second mile.

CONTENTS

PREFACE

Time, measured in any of its artificial units, passes all too quickly and it was only the nudgings of friends which made me collect together some of the poems I have scribbled over the past thirty years. I hope they feel the effort is worth while.

The poems are grouped thematically as far as possible. A few notes are given but on the whole I feel poetry should be able to stand on its own. Too often, these days, muddy obscurity is presented as art. Life is too short for artificial complexities. It is the living that matters, which is why the subjects of time and place, protest and pleas, crop up so often. We have only one life, one world. I mourn the passing of both, even among those most enduring of features, the hills and mountains. Perhaps the natural world looms large in my writings because of the stark contrast with the artificiality of our cities. I grew up as a traveller, a pattern kept going by National Service in Egypt and Kenya, a dozen years pioneering outdoor education and freelancing since as mountaineer and writer. Working on *Poems of the Scottish Hills* really made me gather together my own bits and pieces. I am grateful to Aberdeen University Press and Colin MacLean for their encouragement and also to Ian Strachan for his drawings.

I would also like to thank the BBC and the following publications who have used items over the years: *Aberdeen Press and Journal, ABMSAC Journal, Akros, BFMC Journal, CC Journal, Climber and Rambler, The Countryman, Crusade, Dalesman Publications, Dumfries and Galloway Standard, The Field, Fife Free Press, Footloose, The Great Outdoors, Irish Mountaineering, Lallans, MBA Journal, New Hope International, New Shetlander, Oban Times, Other Poetry, The Scots Magazine, Scotsman Publications, The Scottish Field, SMC Journal, Symphony, Words,* and also Victor Gollancz Ltd for pieces from *Hamish's Mountain Walk* and *Hamish's Groats End Walk*.

Hamish M. Brown
21 Carlin Craig
Kinghorn   1983

COUNTING SHEEP

Sleep is postponed
when words sheep over
the gates of the mind.
It is too late, past dawn,
to gather wool from thorns
and barbed-wire fences.
The beasts have to be grabbed,
dipped and disinfected,
sheared in an hour
while fighting awake
hung-over from day.

Who would be a shepherd
with flocks of words loose
on the fells of the mind
in March moonlight?
I would wash my mind
of the stinking fold,
but I cannot sleep
till I count my sheep.

THE SEASONS

A garden on a winter's day:
Black earth and a pool ice-grey.

A garden with a springtime sigh:
Snowdrop clouds on bluebell sky.

A garden through a summer high--
When no bloom can ever die.

A garden in the autumn run:
Roses pruned and death-frost come.

SNOWFALL

When the first snows come
It is like quiet benediction,
The service over.
We shuffle out, at peace,
Cleansed from civilisation
And the year done.
We look out on drifting purity
As strangers from another age,
Misunderstood.
But whatever our failings, our pity
For a world impoverished, this we know:
That truth has stood.

NOVEMBER GALE

The gale knocked on the door first thing today.
It was scratching and whining like a dog
Trying to get in, away from the beating
Of invisible sticks. It woke me up
And I lay watching it in the grey hour
That's dawn on the Forth at November's end.
Great acres of spray hurled across the sea
Just as heather marks the passage of storm
With waves of wind that surge and sway its slopes
In patterns of moving colour. The sea
Had not half the tints of the mountain slope
But, hill or sea, the glowering sky lowered
Its disapproving brows and cursed day
For banging him from sleep. What we saw there
Was petulance; but a big man angry
Is best walked round. I feared the storm enough
Not to pick a fight, not to stand my ground;
But simply turned over and slept once more
And left the storm to hammer on the door.

WILD GEESE FLYING

Under storm cloudings,
Carefully timed,
The geese fly southwards
In noisy flow.

The voice of the north
(Like winter wind)
Crying the painfulness
Of driven snow.

In white dawn they cried;
While Adam sinned,
Rubbing cold fingers
And watched them go.

Wild wind and weather,
Grey geese that wing,
Do you know the spell
You cast below?

Do you know the longing
That bares the mind,
Icing it nightly
Tight as a bow?

Then blow *me* away!
When geese go past
I am desolate
And winter slow.

ARROWHEADS OF SOUND

Arrowheads of sound,
Flighting, flickering,
Straining, like some flautist
After the perfect note.
  I'd just switched off and gone out
  To let the dog do his thing,
  And post a letter up the hill
  When the sound came, like
  An image in a darkroom tray--
  A magic out of nothingness!
  How vain was the late night news
  And the serial that kept me in.
Arrowheads of sound,
That shot through even my thick skin;
Wild geese, northwards flying, flying,
Forgive this man's world, dying, dying.

SWANS

How does a swan die? How
Lay low, for ever, that snakey neck
And hissing head? How fold cloud wings?
How end the pulsing flight that
Rushes me from bed to count
The spectres passing westwards overhead?
Perhaps they do not die. Perhaps all winds
Are echoes of immortal wings, and clouds
Their feathers dropping from some *Cygnus* paradise.
Death is not the dream we dream with swans,
So we sparrows fly—in them—borrowing their majesty
To match the beatings of our hearts.

REDSHANKS

I was mid-city
midwinter
miles from the sea
when the fog
overhead
cried *pwee wee wee*
pwee wee wee.

It was an echo
of that ghost bird
lives in me.

SPRING

I will escape
From the darkness of the winter.
I will go out
To the colours of the morning.
I will rejoice
In the splendour of life reborn.
I will renew
Faith in the world of God, not man.
I will walk soft
In the slippered hall of the wilds.

RAIN

Rain can soak the soul
as much as soil
and creep through gut
as spectrum oil
on puddles pecked by drops
of nagging wet.

I need no tears of rain
having, in myself,
enough of pain.

But even a crying cynic sees
the rainbow loom,
even a silent sceptic knows
and, late or soon,
against all faith, is won—
kissed on the icy lips of mind
by aberrant sun.

ALL MEN

All men are free under the stars
Yet we bolt our doors and creep to bed,
All men are kings upon the earth
But some have sold their thrones,
despaired, and fled;
All men, in Adam, walked with God,
Now God, and walking, both are odd.

CHOICE

It is on etched hills and lithoed seas
That the stars appear to spin free
About the sky. Freedom is a glance
At the wheeling stars and we
Find that sight by choice, not chance.

PEACE IS A SUNNY DAY

Peace is a sunny day,
hills, and sea.
Would I could find a way
to rest me.

THIS SPRING

Under the basalt dyke this lamb passed death, lies
Faded beyond smell and bone, mere tattered fluff . . .

Which had the harder birth, the shorter breath:
The magma of the weathering Ochils
Or the brief-born lamb lying dead at her feet?

Death is only seconds older than life
It seems, and pain immeasurably old
With the kind hills grown cold, it seems, this spring.

SUNSET

Sunset leaves no footprints on the sand,
Nor shouts goodbye, nor waves her icy hand.
Sunset stands ethereal, a naked body in a pool,
Which we behold as we are made, both wise and fool.
Sunset gives no kisses, lights no star
And all her robing wonders, of our eyes, are.

SIBELIUS, FIFTH

It sweeps the seasons—as wind blows leaves—
And we are stung to wonder with such pain,
Warmed by battle with the notes that freeze,
Made joyous, strange gods, by such rush of rain.
Great forests are all around us, the still waters glint;
We, so soft, clash with his north world, glimpsed,
                                  strong as flint.

A SENSE OF BELONGING

Most at ease among the mountains
For they tell of youth and mystery —
And all men would travel backwards:
The womb is warm!
                    Did you smell the sea?
Did you lie in heather with diamonds overhead?
Or see all secrets in a snowflake?
Did you weep for joy and, in the morning place,
All hungers fill and fearful thirst slake?

THE GOLDEN HILLS

Days without nights,
Days with sunshine that never dimmed
On all our windy way.
We seemed to go
With silver wings that flew us up
Far golden hills of yesterday.

THE THREE FLOWERS

These triplets of the tightly-woven grass
Wink up at dull eyes on many a pass
And force our clumping boots to tread with care —
Or yield guilty excuse to stand and stare.
They add their colours to the machair lawns
These plain worker-flowers, these forgotten pawns
That front chequered boards . . .

Not on the stormy heights, not in the stream,
Not heather-choked, not bog-bound, are they seen,
These common three (blue, yellow, white) —
They favour dry turf, are greedy of light,
And chasten us with their prosaic life and law:
Tormentil,
  Milkwort,
    Lowly bedstraw.

I WILL FIND A MOUNTAIN

I will find a mountain here or there
To act as beacons in the grey
Of civilisation, a brightness in its air
Of gloom.
  God! I would walk into blue day
Above the cold clouds and red strife of men.

It is there we become whole
  — and young again.

THE MOUNTAIN

We have been long years together now;
Secrets fall silent, cares thaw like snow,
We meet as innocents who hand in hand
Can dream a long day past
As one swift hour,
Here's no reserve to open up the heart
Or throw the mantle off the soul,
There is no fear to meet the man and mountain, match
The mountain and the man again.

This is a battle one may fight
And, win or lose, know victory
With clean conquest, purposeness,
This is where man may walk at will
And man be strong as men are meant to be,
This is beauty set alive in dance and song,
This is total art, phoenixed from the rust
And ashes of sophisticated scenes,
This is where the depths of self are found —
On a mountain side.

What madness to the world is this?
Should we not be rebuked and hide
This passion that tingles to the toes
And fingertips of our high being?
This our secret that being glad
To wend our way, to climb our crag,
Our icebound ridge, our summit cone,
That having faced ourselves up there —
The passion must!

THE DOLL

Coming through the Forest of Ae
(which means the far beyond of anywhere)
I suddenly saw an old doll perched on a bank
Beyond the frozen ditch that edged the road.

She had a happy face and I smiled at her.

Perhaps she belonged to some forester,
Some unsure youth who could not bear
To see a childhood memory looking down
From the wardrobe at home. One day
He hid her in his bag and as they
Juddered in to fell beyond the Capel Burn
He threw her from the van; but then,
Walking back, he chanced on her lying
Pink and shamed. In embarrassment he
Propped her up on the slope under the spruce . . .
I can imagine as he daily drives past
He gives a secret smile and wink
To the girl who salutes him from the trees.

I don't know at all of course—these are
Fantasies from my own stepping heart.
But I do know, as I walked past,
The lost doll with her smile winked at me.

CRAIL: THE EBB TIDE

A call! Ah, that old, weird and wasting cry:
The hidden sea-bird in a misty sky.
    Damp dawn but down there the dreary sea calls
    In pulsing, pleading sighs, rises and falls,
    Moves here and there a ghostly glimmer —
    The sleeping tide. The grey gulls gape, flutter
    Weary wings, shuffle in the seaweed scum ...
Turn tired tide—turn with the day that will come.
A call! Then silk silence for the sea lies
Asleep, weary under the sunless skies.

PARADISE RE-VISITED 1981

    I find my peace in
    the Pole Star
    standing above Whitewisp
    for there it stood
    throughout my youth
    a safe constancy
    there it may stand in
    years to come
    when the kind Ochils and I
    have ended—however
    the world ends.

(Paradise is a "secret" spot in the Ochils above Dollar)

MONAIDH LIATH DAWN

We left in the dog hours of dawn's expectancy
When the stars still littered up the dark
Depthlessness of blinded night;
We left in the gasping silence of frozen trees
And crackling footsteps on the grass.
We walked alone.
Each wrapped up in a world his own,
Sheathed in wool and nylon; armoured
To tilt against the day ahead,
Marching with measured tread.

So soon we left the track to stumble up the screes,
Jewelled heather spray, hoary in the dark,
Rising endlessly to meet the bulk and bulge
Of a great buttress—shoulder of the day
And of the first white peak.
We left the misty valley below the stars.
We steamed our own exasperated way
While slowly the day crept in,
Fogging the negative of night
With an unexpected light.

I called to the others so we stopped,
Quietly curled down in the snow,
Wrapped ourselves in wonderment,
(Shivered on earth and sang in heaven)
Gazed over the flooded east
And marvelled at the daily wonder missed
Amid the rumble of the seaside towns
Where the pits spew men and work all day;
Here we watched the cliff shed off the night
To stand pure naked pink in cradle light.

O, the glory of that crimsoned crag at dawn,
And our rough faces reflecting red in turn.
As men would hide their cleanest joys
We blushed. Our inmost hearts were thrilled,
For still it came: great cataracts of spraying light,
Great deluge day, over hills and sky and life
And limbs cramped on the narrow ledge.
The snows faded out. The miracle was past.
We rose, stared over endless ranges, height for height,
Walked on in silence. With cold, full light.

BELAY POINTS

1   'Being there' is enough
We climb,
Tracing a route
Out of time.

2   It's those people
most alive
live most
for their secret prize.

3   Climbers know that life's a bright flower
That grows an inch from death.
You don't have to pick blooms
To enjoy their scent.

CAMP BY THE BUACHAILLE

So freely Glencoe gave those early joys:
the rasp of porphyry
beneath finger tips,
the peppery sweetness
of blaeberry
on purpled lips,
the scarves of clouds
round mountain ridge,
the snowing cotton grass
by Coupal Bridge,
the numbed pale hands
of a winter climb,
May evening air
like cool white wine ...

The pleasures have not dulled with dusting years:
the whispering wetness,
sighing moonlight,
wind's caresses,
young stars peering round
the Crowberry Tower,
the shiver of greenshanks' calling
through dawn's silk hour,
the fangs of Cruachan,
hazed hints of sea,
dewdrops,
butterwort, tangy myrtle,
tormentil,
the flowers of frozen grass —
the little things of the long content
born of that brooding pass.

GLENCOE CAMEO

I desire the high place:
The place of sun-touched night,
Of the veil of mist arising
And eagled wings of light,
Of red crags of Bidean,
The blackness of The Ridge
And a late splash in the river
Below the bridge.

C. I. C. DEPARTURE

At six we stood coldly on the snow,
wondered why
we'd left our bunks, the comfort of the hut,
for an icy sky.
Within?
     Warm walls of wood,
sleep, blanket-deep, dream-drugged —
lazy delight . . .

but we cramponed off before the stars
burned out of the northern night.
Ahead?
     A new route of our wanting, wanting, lay.
Its price our early exodus,
our joy in matching day.

THE MOUSE

The dog, dancing on snowy slopes,
Pounced on a mouse.
One squeal and it was dead.
But the dog was bitten (his nose) and bled
So the squeaking snows that day were sprinkled
with stuttering spots of red.

That night I dreamed of death again —
But under Garadh Gully the stain spread.
We gathered up a broken friend
And saw the bannered headlines
About a tragic end.

So we made the weather our excuse
And stayed in bed.

THE HARLOT

Ben Nevis is a mountain
Of loveless loveliness.
Like a fat woman she broods,
cold-shouldered of warm romance,
too drunken for gentle kiss.
Love has just scratched her. She reeks
like a discarded garment.

As so many cold hundreds
have pissed against the cairn,
she is soiled through and wet
and weary in her solitude.

Yet it is to this harlot
the generations come—brash boys
to test their nascent lusts,
a giggle that so often has an echoed death.

I have come to hate the bitch.

The sterile heart of her is stone
and her smile is slimy ice.
We should have heeded the old advice:
not all snowy frills—or hills—are nice.

HIGHLAND PEBBLES

At the mouth of the Spey
I collected pebbles
carried from the hills
and tumbled
so they were ready to mount
with only half a week
of the cerium oxide.
They look well on the skin
of the right girl.

I wonder if she can guess
the million years
she carries at her neck?

On An Teallach
the red sandstone
is embedded with pebbles too
and here and there
they litter the ground
like a spilled bag of sweets.
They too were tumbled
(but at creation's dawn),
carried beyond all rivers
to the world's first sea.

The ocean heaved up
to form great hills
and from the disintegration
of those mountains
the quartz pips were pushed aside
from the pudding rock.
They too tumble well
and, mounted, make
delicate jewellery.

When I placed my offering
on her neck my gentle kiss
had double wonder:
of her, and this.

SLIOCH

(the Gaelic translates as *the spear*)

Slioch was the arena
Slioch the wild beast
Slioch the spear.

On Christmas Day
It was thumbs up
Though the snows
Showered neither victors
Nor vanquished.

We paraded in awe
Our temerity gaining
Icy applause.
The cheers were
within us.

The red sunset
Wrote blood on the hill.
Those cheers suffice
For memory lasts
And we had our will.

Slioch was the arena
Slioch the wild beast
Slioch the spear.

THE HILL OF THE SPEAR

Slioch may be *the spear*
but its defences were weak
against the raiding centuries.

A million years armed the peak,
set it, moated, in the wilds —
a citadel of clouds,

but a mere millenium marched
with axe and fire and paper swords
to write the end of old songs.

Scissors cut paper but hard rock
smashes scissors, only to find
paper power the greatest of foes.

The title deeds of time disarmed
honour and loyalty. Slioch, *the spear*
is broken. Now it is just a hill.

SANDWOOD

Light echoes to light in the day-held night
Where I camp by the sea.
                              My spurting fire
Sparkles its stars to pale, reflective skies . . .

Here is one secret place! On the rim, north,
And most, it is me.
                              Peace never lies.

TARFSIDE

The Hill of Rowan has a cross on its heart
cut in grey stone
on a purple tweed of ling.
Up there, as the old years stotter by,
the young birds sing.

I have walked so many foreign miles through life
but cannot regret
green years that have, somehow, gone.
Now, I lean on the gate, to listen, listen --
still hear that song.

A SALTING OF SNOW

The farmer said,
"Just a salting of snow" —
an odd way of putting it
for salt and snow we usually see
in the mess of busy streets.

But it was apt,
with the fawn haunches of the Howgills
spread with the salt-snow
and nicely grilling in a winter sun
set at a low number.

We raised the dust of it
as we tramped the white fells
the short day through.
Just a salting of snow,
but enough to flavour
the day so the ordinary
turned into a feast.

RETREAT

Before us the clouds
camouflaged the mountains and cwms
in erratic tones —
a frantic preparing for battle
which we, hopefully neutral,
could have done without.
Before Llyn Ogwen the hail
shot its bullets at our backs
and the Carneddau rumbled bigger guns.
We fled!
       Down, to our mobile column,
safe from the 'orrible 'ills,
down the A5, suddenly full
of August refugees,
to make our peace in "The Cock & Bull".

BRANDON

Do you remember Brandon,
Our mountain in the west:
Brandon that looks on oceans,
Brandon of the blessed?

Do you remember Brandon
In hoary frost that day
With Smerwick heather burning
and curraghs in the bay?

Do you remember Brandon
And marching pilgrim feet,
The blowing mists around us
Where saints and sinners meet?

Do you remember Brandon
With staff in youthful fist,
The turf reek in our nostrils,
Hair silvered by the mist?

Do you remember Brandon
When still too young to talk
And do you mind the conquest
When first we made the walk?

Do you remember Brandon
(the *aire-cnoc gear* a jibe)
When we could climb all mountains
And love a girl beside?

Do you remember Brandon,
Our swim in Nalacken,
And the first pint in Dingle
When we returned as men?

Do you remember Brandon
When penitence was real
And hearts knew true devotion
To follow that ideal?

Do you remember Brandon,
Brandon of the blessed,
Brandon that looks on oceans —
Sad tideway to the west?

Do you remember Brandon,
A lifetime now away.
The oath we took on leaving
To lie by Brandon Bay?

Do you remember Brandon?
It's there I think to fly
While yet there is tomorrow —
For Brandon, and goodbye.

BALLYDAVID, BY GALTYMORE

Ballydavid, by Galtymore,
That is the place to rest you now!

Under the historian's oak --
A colour burst among the pines
That ambush the long descent
From the turf-edged, booleying heights
Of O'Loughman's Keep.

There's a high spring on Galtymore.
From it I've heard young laughter race its slopes --
Tripping from green and golden fields
That mile to Tipperary town
Beyond the Vale of Aherlow.

Such crimson years that oak has known
To give to us such benison.
Sure all life is a mountainy road!
Peace then, for this corner of it --
And the big view.

Ballydavid, by Galtymore,
That is the place to rest you now!

A SOMEWHERE

I could show you a somewhere, sad and old,
So like a woman with her prinkled face,
White-faded from childhood's gold,
Arthritic in pace,
Spirits cold . . .
Yet once she was the darling of the class
And that was the prettiest of any place.

GLEN ORCHY, CAMPING

Rain sounds so much wetter
When your roof is nylon
— six inches overhead —
and the wind from the west is blowing.

But it's clean and better
Than home's glass-loud patter
— the urban chemistry —
when the smoke from the works is snowing.

PITCH SEVEN

It is consummation, a mad rape
Of earth's solid resisting; mute
Limbs thrusting, hands grasping,
Minds godworn, craving a primitive substitute.

It is not
Behaviour as was always there!
Outworn creeds, too simple
For our fractured, shackled, nightmare understanding.
We were content once, or dreamt we were,
Before the plastic age
Before the bomb
Before free love
Free milk
Free doom.

Agag no longer tip-toes
Tripping with a virgin wonder,
Jericho's walls are broken down
For glory, death and plunder.

It is substitution, a dagger desperation
Ripping bare the nakedness of men.
Why?

Because we must
Engage the body to liberate the mind,
Embrace earth rock to find a soul.

It is all the deep things of long ago
Swept away, then phoenix born
For a new generation.
We may not understand, God knows,
But still we climb.

Take in the tangled slack!

NOR MOUNTAINS WAIT

I envy solitude
and silence among the coloured hills.
I envy wind and stars
and all the gossamers of life
that man can see but cannot touch
or rule, or legislate.
Waves are not asked to queue,
Nor mountains wait.

CASTLERIGG

"Permissive Paths" and Motorways
(these waymarks of our lemming life)
mean little in the tramp of time —
                    I think.
I saw young Castlerigg dance round a ring,
Look up to old Skiddaw with his kin —
                    and wink.

MODERN MOUNTAINEERING

We used to wander in the park,
We used to lie at ease,
A hopeless situation
That cannot hope to please.
They've put a big band in the stand
And deck chairs on the grass,
Amusements line the quiet paths,
It's murder trying to pass.
There's Mods and Rockers in the hall —
Some foreign conference too —
Demands for education
Have broken up the Zoo.
"It's us, the mighty multitude,
We want our heroes tall.
Dance the way we indicate,
Or hell, don't dance at all.
Love is common property.
We'll burn the shrubbery!
Life's a played-out game today,
Outworn with puberty.
Leisure must be litigated,
Secrets must be expressed.
We're out to build . . . "
A plastic age —
If only you had guessed.
So love is done by numbers now
And climbing is the same.
O give me back the mountains
Before the climbers came.

MOUNTAINS ARE A MAGIC

Mountains are a magic
to confound
the plodding sceptic
in his round.

Mountains are a madness
to make well
a world living close
by to hell.

Mountains are a sorrow
too soon past
but gold in the soul
while we last.

RAIN AT KINCRAIG

The rain is uncertain, whiskers
A tentative route to the cruel earth,
It nuzzles the dust, trailing it
With mousey prints, scurrying tracks.
It scrabbles at the rocks and tears
A wainscot patter through the trees
And then, as if assured, casts off
The uncertainties of the weak,
It shivers up reserve forces
And with the big guns thundering
Through the cowering world goes plundering.
It's only at the end of storm,
When the floods fall back and winds go
That the scurrying rain retreats
By little whispers to its roots.

I HAVE A DOG

I have a dog who loves me, loves me
      — and I love him.

There's a difference in our love, our love
      — he has no sin.

DOGS

We humans talk
Of treating other
Humans as dogs;
But my dumb beast
Treats me as a dog,
Thank God.

RONAS HILL

Sullen Sullom Voe
is visible,
seen from the chambered cairn
on Ronas Hill.
There is always wind,
always wind,
blowing in the mind
on Ronas Hill.
Are all summits hollow,
man-empty,
marking our beginning,
marking our end?

SEEN FROM YELL

We were wind-warmed.
Rain knocked on windows
like ideas wanting in.
Across the sound and over the braes
the loom of Sullom Voe spat
an obscene moonscape
among the real clouds
of the simmer dim.
The camps of the self-slaved
were un-naturally bright —
neon writing with
a full stop red up on the hill.

ASPHODEL

Best of hill flowers
Is the regal asphodel
That ends our summer
By catching stars, setting them
On wands among the moors.
They burn brighly, gold
And yellow shoots of fire
Which leaves dry parchment prayers
Stark on the stalks of winter.
Only when the new-minted stars
Are gathered from translucent skies
Of blue summer
Can the pale princes burn;
For one month sceptres stud the moor —
And asphodel is king.

EYE OF THE WIND

This is one of those kind ships,
A ship which took smiling seas
Deep into the hearts of friends
To sail them from dreams to daring,
Doing that which has no regretting
When the final port looms its light
And we sail in, to our goodnight.

SAILING OFF

Hold, sun, for just another hour of day!
We know pale dusk's when all ships weigh
And sail off; and the last sunset
May be best of all — but not just yet.
I have a thousand miles to travel, friend;
Then sail me under, make a glorious end.

NIGHT DUTY

There is a cruel chillness in the desert air.
There always is!
And though my tiredness swings like a lighted flare
And shadows sway a dream-mad dance
                                    I am not alone.

There are long hours of duty waiting yet.
There always are!
And though my bleary eyes watch the moon set
And the faint, lonely haze of dawn
                                    I am not alone.

HOME: FROM THE DESERT

There is a wild will in the wind. It wings,
Sending sea-spray skying. Spirited, it sings
Round the walls
And it falls
To puff the smoke and rattle window panes.
It is winter. They laugh quiet inside. HOME!

There is a sad sigh in the breeze that slips
And sidles out between the burning lips
Of fierce day.
Sweat away —
While slowly the shimmered shine of sun gains
Intensity. Drudgery's day-dream: HOME!

GO I MUST

Into the haze of the heat and dust
I will go for go I must.
There are no cool waves lapping here
And sighing winds are lost, aloft, in fear.

Through the gate the camel goes, and comes,
Perhaps in the memory a city hums
And we remember green parks, a lover's kiss,
Deep grey clouds from tall smoking chimney towers ...
It seems a mirage! Face again to this,
For the desert calls for the future hours!

Into the desert I go, for go I must,
Into the haze of heat and dust.
Plunge beast! March! The sun is yet to set,
And set? We drive on our journey yet.

THE COMING OF SLEEP

The desert has drowned the careless sun. Rest
Comes slowly: cull-creeping like the stars lest
(Tripping chance)
It should glance
The memory into painful things of old
To shatter like icicles hung unkind.

Shatter not. Scatter not. Let me lie deep
Down in mellow memory. Let me sleep
The sleep which
Stars bewitch
And send the snow-soft falling of the cold
Surroundings into nothing. Age will remind.

SUNSET: IN MEMORIAM

The glinting remains are where wild winds moan,
Where those four swift winds, repassing, swept away
(And later on returned to their home)
Leaving the candid face of the desert — grey.

Though drawn the covering, though she weep,
Her tears sparkle in the high above;
The strength of men tired, must fall asleep.

That sun, sent down daily off the lowest desert side,
Drags a curtain of time about her face;
But here, where the crusted mind will slide,
Far her strength must, unuplifting, race.

Her heights of mid-day were only decreed
That she the night of panic freed
By tumbling like a clown. Down! Creep
And grovel in the dust of deserts blown.
That which was born is now welcomed home.

DEVERSOIR: THE DIVE

The light, long-known lift of the toes,
A flight, then brokenly the brilliant world goes
Spinning in shimmered topaz lights above
While fiery fishes fly . . .
        O swiftly move,
Swiftly, silently, like a bird flung out
To fly forever. There is the old shout
Of triumph in the pounding heart and long
Reach of the arms. O God! The body is strong,
Free in nakedness, born of the cool chill,
Born of fantasy, born of liquid thrill.

44

Where is the world?
        And where the man who lies
Gasping on the Suez sands with the cries
Of peddling children calling in their ears?
Sten guns lie, lifeless as thoughts and fears.
This is a new world!
        A Kingdom! God gave
It for peace. So meaningless -- man's one wave.

Dive! There is nothing of man.
        The fish flash
In all their rainbow raiment. Free; they dash
Between the blue and golden pillars. Free;
They are themselves a oneness with the sea.

Ten seconds, twenty, thirty; briefly I
Am one of them; until I give a cry
And buckle in my fate.
        Singing in ears;
Explosive lungs give vent. All the deep fears
Come rushing, rasping like the waters in
My nose. Gone the green, glancing glitter. Swim!
Poor panicked person. What right had you there
To live one minute from your natal air?

Joy. Strength still stands! For when each choking lung
Is calm again, laughing, I shall be flung
Dancing deep down into the salty sea.
Alive: I smile, I sing, I hold my breath,
                I dive.

THE AIRMAN'S LETTER

No, it is not the opaque and orange moon I dream about
tonight.
Here, though the weak whispers of the waves are wimping
on the sands,
My mind is far away . . .
       I dream of soft and silvered snowlight:
Shining like the stars splattered in frosty fistfuls on that
land.
Blame me not for wandering!
       Out here the sands sting, stab hell-hot,
Here, the lonely, only streams are tickling trickles sweating
slow
Down the worn, warm, brown-deep-skin, off grimy arms,
to leave a blot
On a painfully penned "epistle". (Written on the mock-
white-snow
Of cheap, chewed, Signals Section paper)
       Oh, how I long for cold,
Cloying clouds. And mystic mists. For high home hills.
                    Beautiful. Bold.

A DREAM OF JERUSALEM

O, for the shock of the Arab world
With the sting of the sand in the air,
For the dusty road and the camel path
And the play of the sun in the hair.

O, for the smell of the sweet-meat stalls,
The busy shops in The Chain,
The chatter of a thousand tongues —
Like Pentecost again!

O, for the night on the rooftops there
With the stories running wild,
Or the sight of the city at dawn
And the smile of a passing child.

For the tramp of the Legion men at dusk
And their wild cry from the wall
And the last farewell on the Bethany road
Where the cyprus stand so tall.

THE CHILD OF THE KYRENIA HILLS

I want to go up to the hills again
Where the rock-roses scent soft midnight air.

I want to go up to the hills again
To feel the moonbeams play upon my hair.

I want to go up to the hills again
To follow the stars run above the trees.

I want to go up to the hills again
To chase cloud-creatures in whispering leaves.

I want to go up to the hills again
For the living God is close on the height.

I want to go up to the hills again
For innocence again—my youth's last night.

SAVE MY BOY

Take me,
Take my mother;
Of her giving, take my brother,
Even whisper, take my wife,
But save my boy:
My boy yet growing unalarmed,
Save him who has not harmed,
Save my boy!

My boy *was* saved;
But war came round again,
Like conkers in the autumn —
A seasonable game.
Then his life was broken,
His future torn apart,
Scattered in the street
As brown leaves blown.

I reap, I reap,
The seed I've sown.

REQUIEM

Let us be now. Let us be.
What more would you have of me?
Let us sleep under the growing grass;
The wintered war, God, let it pass.
We did not ask for praise,
(That belongs to the living of men's days)
We did not ask for this.
Some bullets were not made to miss.
There is no glory in death:
It comes and goes like winter breath.
You that are left must bear the loss;
We did not find it hard, the brook to cross.

O God, I have a little son. He cries.
It is there that the soldier dies:
Before the battle, before the din.
I kissed him sleeping. Requiem.

JUNE SUNRISE, KENYA

O Lord grant this that I may lie
And watch the swallows in the sky.
Give me an hour of rest from this cruel tie
And I shall laugh until I dance and cry.

I cry for the beauty of the hills I see
Where careless clouds sail soft for me.
O what a fresco God's finger set free —
Thus was it said--and thus the world shall be.

There the silver clouds leave sleeping to the night,
For dawn is lifting high her light.
Sure from some glory of primeval flight --
It glints on the wing—and mine the delight.

How swift to the light is the bird of today,
How cool the dew, how soon away.
And I shall sleep, perchance to dream the lay:
The bird in the cloud, the gold in the hay ...

CHRISTMAS EVE, NAIROBI

I can lift up eyes to green fields
And gentle skies --
How our hearts rejoice. The soul reels,
Memory cries . . .

Gone. Long hours in the desert waste.
Gone forever.
See. Buds are bursting; O make haste --
Bloom forever.

Run footsteps over grassy slopes
Singing with bees;
Lift past blue trees the breathless hopes,
Follow the breeze.

Set eyes upon the golden sky:
My Christ is born.
Forget the aircraft drone and fly
This passing storm.

The sun is smiling and beckons;
Life is for good.
When I pass it will not slacken --
Laughter has stood.

IN JOSHIMATH

Sheep and peewits and the weepy wind,
These are the things that creep to mind.
   In the greater hills, the sterile snows,
   We long for home—where memory flows,
   Where dream-sight tumbles the stars on the grass
   And phantoms go tramping up to the pass ...
The hills where we ran, young with zest,
Are best when, returning, we seek our rest.

IN MEKNES

It is in hot Meknes I sit, sipping
A glass of *thé citron*,
But in my mind I sit with ghosts
In Zermatt or by Rhône.

A shaded Martigny *pâtisserie* perhaps,
Or a pool of green dreams, with many
Mountains climbed—each a glad sojourn
In youth's sweet surety, seeing the corn
Years golden, on and on ...

Now, through heat-sweeping day, in pale mirage
I see all those faces, all those joys,
All those years—all gone. All gone.

SUNSETS

(i. m. Steve Biko)

When the sunset burned the snow
It stoked a wrath of memory.
I looked, not over a splendid world,
One man on his million-acre peace,
Not at my freedom eagled in the sky,
Not at love soft as spindrift silk . . .
I saw blood in the red, and sweat,
And tears, for wars still to be waged
Before man can walk the heights clear
Of sharp, cramponing conscience.

It is so easy to admire sunsets on Ben More.
Would I rise to such admiration in Soweto say?
I doubt it. That sort of superiority isn't mine.
To admire sunsets under those circumstances
Is to have scaled heaped Everests of fire.

THE SUN SHINES AT TAROUDANT

It is warm comfort in this western squall
As the rain blasts my tiny tent
To know, with longing, that old thrall
— the sun shines now at Taroudant.

Morocco lies a million dreams away
And freedom is a bad debt, lent-
Coin for those who, so wilful say
— the sun shines now at Taroudant.

I pack and struggle through the hills,
Wet and weary, yet gladly spent,
Carried by my dream knowledge:
— the sun shines now at Taroudant.

IN THE SOUKS

The magic markets in dusty Marrakech
Have not altered in a thousand years.
Even though through them creeps a tourist crocodile
Their secrets are safe. The joys, the tears,
Are chameleon bones and hoopoe skins.
Verily, visions are not bought and sold.
The souks are an illusion. Man dares
Put himself to auction—and trades his wares.

DESCENT FROM THE MATTERHORN

Meadows of life: living, juicy scents;
Calm colours mingling as in clouds;
Waters that sprayed rainbow shocks
Of tiny clammy hands.
                    Alive!
Cow bells; warm fly-loved life;
Church bells; our kith and kin —
People, as dead, walking unawares;
Golden plums, pulp trickling down a chin.
God! After the thunderstorm, so close to death,
Life's bedlam was a welcome sound —
Even gaudy Breuil was joy
(Though under the *pension* rafters our heads beat
With a pulsing lust) Life?
                    Life,
Borrowed in the storm, bold life
Was handed mellow to our youth again.
Saxifrages starred the stones and scree
And a flurry of flowers flecked the grass.
As we came down, alive, from the Matterhorn.

ALPINE REST DAY

I have lain all day at Châtelleret,
The wall of the Meije above:
Immovable wall of black and white
Slicing the cool clouds through.
This much may we rest;
Then Promontoire
And thence the long upsurge
With hands and feet and heart at ease
In a dawn of splendid fire.

It is much easier lying near-naked in the sun
With icy melt-water bright on the skin,
It is much easier listening to the marmot's cry,
Finding a soldenella,
It is much easier—but still we go
To the sunlit rock and the glacier glow.

O God, the daphnia scent is strong!

We saught this—retreat—from the world outside:
Down that long valley we'd walked, and bussed another,
Aye, crossed a continent, a channel and another land.

What are they doing at home?

The others have come up. We'll eat. Then sleep.
Then Promontoire. The Meije.
The sun. The flowers. The content of a dizzy dream.
The next challenge lies so very mountainous ahead.
It is not easy:
So soon from bed.

BY ZION

Jerusalem in silence!
And I had imagined in my heart a sad,
soft, almost sickly singing.
The very stars have echoed with mad,
sobbing notes,
    shouting*:*
        Crucify!

Jerusalem in silence!
So much imagined, but in the air a song
(glad, almost golden singing)
with voices (cool as moonlight) rising up
past Kedron,
    crying:
        Arisen!

NORTH WIND

North Wind, North Wind,
Pluck a cloud for me;
Shake it over sinners
For Nativity.

North Wind, North Wind,
Paint the starry trees,
Show us how to worship
As cattle on their knees.

CHRISTMAS TREES

"The snow fairy-lights the trees
like Christmas decorations."
What a vain, man-proud simile
seeing trees were bright like this before Christ
or Christmas came to earth.

These snows are stars, and worlds, heaped
in worship of that birth.
White truth however is apt to end
decking out man's plastic trees.

That men adorn trees, dear God,
is wild, divinest irony:
the snow virginity of Bethlehem
crucified in spruce
on Calvary Hill.

JESUS

Light as the dawning
And bright as the sun,
Thus was His calling
And thus had He run.
Swift as the dawning
And brighter than day,
Thus was His calling,
His marking the way.

HE CAME

He came in the bustle of Galilee —
The Cross for the Child, the Tomb for the Truth;
And how can I hide, for he came for me?

Who pierced His heart till the blood ran free,
Pierced the strong feet and the hands that had healed?
And how is my pain—for He came for me?

THE MOONLIT VALLEY

The future lies like a moonlit valley;
Full of shining shapes, of shadows,
Of mystery and magic, hopes and fears . . .
O, the glory of that valley!
For down it, softly, the Son of God goes,
Reconnoitering all the unknown years.
I go to see the country He will take.

A JOURNEY TO MAKE

I have a journey to make
Beyond the shores of time.
I have a journey to make
Which only can be mine.

Will I make it in fine array
With banners in my van,
For we must make of journeys
Whatever proof we can?

Will I make it singing, glad,
My youth made strong,
Or will it be a murmured thing,
An old and broken song?

It frightens me to hoist a sail
Or foot a mountain way,
Yet the journey comes to every man
As night becomes the day.

BEYOND STARS

We fix our aim on a distant star
To wing our way across the sky;
Reaching out to a goal so far
Our souls shall never, ever die.
There, through one star see others shine
And know that we are nothing, yet!
Those others. On and on. They're mine,
For the sun of stars shall never set.

IMPOTENCE

We have a clock which chimes once
On the half hour, a brief resonance
In the night hours that leaves me
Wondering at the time. Half past what?
Half past life perhaps and the hope I strike
Reverberates on the cold night of a world
Deeply asleep and unaware.

THE QUEST

In the distant mountains
I had sought for rest,
Looked to them for something
Of our human best;

But the quest was fruitless.
Man is not a god,
Nor the ground made sacred
Where by chance he trod.

In the hope of springtide
Hides the winter breath,
And the gate of heaven
Opens, once, by death.

Seek it not on mountains
Nor upon the sea,
The hope of all mankind
Hangs upon a tree.

EVENING STAR

At evening, or the last dark night,
We are glad of stars—telling all
The thousands who have gone before:
Pilgrims standing in solemn hall.

Each star tells an ancestral night;
But man was set to march by day
And pilgrims know no easy door —
Come evening star, gold turns to grey.

We stand the pilgrims on the height:
Thirsty and ragged, such tired men . . .
But faith takes us through, so lower
Portcullis stars—we've won by then.

PEACE

Peace is not the absence of noise
And the tramping of many feet,
Peace is not just mountain summits
At the end of a frantic week.
Peace is within, like blood or gut
And as simple and strong as stone,
Peace is the soul's circulation,
The atonement within the bone.

DEATH

Do not say "he now has rest"
when death's touch
has merely closed my eyes.
Rest became a habit long ago
and death's no black surprise.
Weep tears—of joy—my friends, for me.
My beginning is in my end.

BRACKEN

Which is more dead: the bracken underground
Held sleeping by winter frost
Or bracken uncurled, painted green,
By the bold summer breezes tossed?

Don't talk of death while such renewal shows
Its colours to the hill tops.
Into the spores on the wind blows the life
That will bud when ours has stopped.

AFTER

Will we, in the grave,
feel the weight of the earth?
reel under the pressure of hill,
stars, and sea?
They have so long carried me
it seems only fair, when I lie there,
to feel the pulse of soil and air.

I WOULD DRINK

I saw beauty in a tall pine tree
And wonder in a cloudy sky;
Peace was like the waters' flow and I
Would drink so deep, would walk so free.

TIME

Time, which we grasp (though it will fly),
is quicksilver in the end:
not to be saved, not to lend,
but thrown, like rain, into the sky.

ECHOES

"Why are you so beautiful?"
I shouted on the mountainside
And the boastful echoes answered:
    "So beautiful so beautiful ... "

"Why are you always peaceful?"
And I tiptoed in my stride
To catch the disturbing whisper:
    "Always peaceful always peaceful ... "

"Are you never, ever, silent?"
(For I sought a place to hide)
The words came over the water:
    "Ever silent ever silent ... "

The echo lied.

WE HAD A WORLD ONCE

We had a world once, they say,
Of green and fruitful things
But man has reaped his whirlwind
And no bird sings.

We had a people once, I hear,
Made in image of God.
What is this name? And who were they?
Where had they trod?

With five limbs and a monster's head
I cannot comprehend.
We sterile remnant, so I'm told,
Lived through The End.

WHEN THEY DROP THE BOMB

When they drop
the bomb
try to be close
to its hit;
it's the best place to be:
you die quick.

MUSHROOMS

As a child there was wonder
in the mushroom rings
that appeared overnight,
white mushrooms that quietly
map-pinned the fields
below the mill
so we went out laughing
to dance our dawn.
We were giants!
Our life towered
over mushroom worlds
and peopled them
with dreams and watered them,
in the end, with tears
for the city spread over the fields.

Last night on television
they discussed nuclear blasts,
showed us a map, dotted
with rings where the missiles fall
to destroy us all.
And each had a symbol —
a mushroom cloud.
They showed the blinded kids
and the rotting death
the survivors face.
They showed our leaders
burrowing into the ground
to escape the spores —
postponing their end
for when this mushroom grows
there is no seed
to grow any more
children, and the fields
will lie black
in the sterility of death
mushroomed
over the world.

IRISH HEDGEROW

Fuchsias, that blazed in a wall of red,
Drenched in the dewy, first-tears of day,
Now drop, one by one, as a summer bled,
Life, in the showers, washed quite away.
Such momentariness in beauty's kiss —
Flowers bleed on the ground. Life comes to this.

FLEDGELINGS

What drives the young bird from its tight, warm nest
into tossing chance?

Man goes to his long toil girded, mysteriously,
in like circumstance.

But tell me, does the mocking bird look back, with pain,
For that security man knows no more again?

ON THE SEASHORE

I scribbled my name on the sand
And the sea had its say.
Old time is washing out the land —
And I have had my day.

I made my paper boats and launched
Them on the rushing tide.
They never returned where they were placed —
And I have pain inside.

The sun on the sea lies weeping,
Day on our shore is done,
Soon the wandering world is sleeping —
The sighing of stars has come.

The sun on the sea lies weeping.
The child has gone to rest;
And a man his dream is dreaming —
Of the years that were best.

I AM AN ECHO

I am an echo
born out of vaginal walls of stone
thrown like a pebble
or a bubble blown blown blown

I am a shadow
that meets its fear on the wall
broken windows
that show nothing at all all all

I am that empty view
the horizon that forgot to bend
foam in the falls
a start looking for an end end end.

EGO SUM

I am a bird
Sings all the spring
Then in autumn
Can't raise a wing.

I am a flower
Blossoming bright
But the wind blows
Dead in the night.

I am a wave
Touching the shore
Then ebbing out
To flow no more.

I am a cloud
One moment there
Next moment gone
Into cold air.

I am a star
So high so high
That when I wink
My light will die.

TIME FOR BAT AND BALL

Time for bat and ball,
To sit against a wall,
To dream.
To scream,
To clipe,
To fight;
But time for all,
Time, time for all.

Time to beck and call,
No bloody time at all;
Just work
Or shirk,
Be wed
And fed,
Retirement and a pall --
Time! No time at all.

SLEEP

I fall asleep to meet my dream
In clear and easy mind
And would that waking,
Waking,
Were half as kind.

Dreams are like the chorus of birds,
A marvel uncontrolled
And would that singing,
Singing,
I woke as bold.

Or as lit waters bright and gold
Or black as they are deep.
Ah, would that plunging,
Plunging,
I dived through sleep.

A. B.

A gentle lapping by the salty flags,
A plaintive cry among the desert crags
Crags, I loved!
Flags, I moved
In wild acres of air, savannahs of space
To follow her footsteps. Ambushed at the start
And led on like wildfire—she set my feet to race.
But the Bitter Lake took all: her hope, my heart —
Flames of love quenched before flesh consumed.
Petals strewn before the flower bloomed.

AND SING NO MORE

All down our days, now long ago,
Love warmed our timeless youth.
I sang my love, ran miles of joy. We fanned
Strong fires of faith.
                         O truth.
O innocence. Fate found the score.
Now I blow ashes—and sing no more.

LOST LOVE

Love, lost, is still a silence
Wrung
By time into no sharing,
Sung
Secretly as a mountain blackbird gives
One
Brief chorus: scree-sharp, brittle, faltering,
Done.

HER WALL

So we touch lives—and break them too
Like ice on puddles where we tread.
Fierce joys are like sunsets:
Black night from red.

So we drink joy—but drunkards lie
Till morning's brute reality
When soberness awaits
Disgustingly.

So we live off—so we die on,
Worldly-wise in our own conceit,
Refusing ever to
Admit defeat.

So we write songs—and sing them too,
Breaking the heart's voice note by note.
But still the mountain stands,
It never spoke.

IN THE RUT

The summer pipers have flickered
wings off to Africa
their singing spent.
Only a penny robin limps a tune
on a garden wall —
an echo of the lusts of spring,
green season of the birds.

Red autumn belongs to antlered hearts,
to those who would woo
through rain and frost
and snow their passion on the hills.
What toys birds are when stags roar
and roar their month-long rage
of thunderstorm
and waterfall
combined.

There is a remnant of respect
in our plastic observation
of sinewy beast.
He has the power to gralloch our past
and remind us of heathery origins
and cave man doubts.
He is our hoary past, breathing clouds
of frosty fear into the clean air
we live without.

Stags are the nearest to gods we have,
the nearest to the oldest
stalking hopes of man.
When we hear stags bellow on the open strath
we are shut in to centuries
forgotten, rutting the centuries
up to now
till we stand in all-modern pride,
stiff with self-congratulation
at our species.

I would have stayed a stag.

DISTURBING HINDS

One bark.
The piston heads shoot up
To periscope the hill.

They kneel up,
Grudgingly,
Gout-minded,
Try a few steps ...

An old bitch gives a snort.

The righteous congregation
Of successionist pride runs --
High-headed,
Panic hidden in upturned noses,
Presbyterian goosestep.

They pause on a ridge
For a last look
That leaves no doubt
About what they think of us;

Carry their caudal contempt
Out of sight.

THE ROBIN'S SONG

There is a robin singing on the wall.
The other robins challenge to his call,
To them it is a cry: stark, defying trespass.
Too bad! Yet who would wish to clip his wings?
The red robin knows just that—and sings!

A SMALL SPACE

I inhabit
such a small space
in the middle
of birling space
you would think
our appointed powers
would let me be
for a couple of hours.
But they hound us all
from birth to death
and it is sin
to draw a breathe
or stop
or think.

NORTHERN TRANQUILLITY

O, it's tranquil here, the poet said —
And the dead agreed with him.
There's peace here, peace so deep
It's opaque as the simmer dim.
Go eat tranquillity who sings its praise
And see how many stones pale peace will raise.

O, it's hard work, the fisherman knows
(And the nets are cleared by a firm brown hand),
The soil is thin and the wind is woe
And men are broken by the grey-green land.
Yet there is tranquillity, and their heart is strong.
Love is stronger than death. And life gangs on.

BY KEIL RUINS, MUCK

The sun sets (bled from a summer's day)
Over the dark steel of Canna's prow.
Its colour is wet with hopelessness —
Such as was born from these sad grey stones
That hide their faces in the grass.

"Camp up there among the dead houses --
If the haunted village gives you peace ... "
Would I were haunted!
        Would the stones could weep!
If only I could soothe some restless past
Perhaps, then, I too could sleep.

GLEN DESSARRY

I have been here before I feel,
Like a wind that circles a hill
And in its own self catches peace —
A memory, still.

Could an ancestor reach a hand
To take mine, by the old march cairn,
Just as, last summer quietly gone,
I led my own bairn?

These hills hint no fear from their past.
They are "home", as to ling, or deer;
But when I look past my son's sons
It is then I fear.

EXTINCTIONS

I

Wouldn't it be nice to have some real snow:
A careless, modern, whitewash job rather
Than a touched-up Brueghel with its detail
Sharp as his dogs' bark. Obliteration.
That is what we deserve, to clean the stain
That we have created on our own earth.
The horror is that man himself could send
The silencing snows. And some day he will.

II

He was walking so damn confidently,
Striding along the road like a new king
Off to a military review. Black ice
Is no respecter of persons. We laughed
To see great dignity sat on its ass.
But who will laugh when our arrogant world
Takes its last spin? I doubt it will be a
Dignified falling. It's too big a death.

III

Prepare to Meet Thy Doom the boards declare
In lettering antique as the words and
The bearer kin to Moses with his beard —
And the boards heavy as Sinai itself.
The cinema queue shuffles in, to watch
Its dreams masquerade. Would it not be just
If one night they came out and found Moses
And all the others set on either hand
With the Almighty laughing at his joke?

BEASTS WILD AND TAME

It's not the *wild* that haunts and hunts —
The raw predation's by the tame.
('Urban Sprawl Slaughters Skylark Song',
Not the poor hawk of evil name.)
Perhaps man talks of nature red
To hide the scarlet of his shame.

PICKING OX-EYE DAISIES

In this narrow summer lane I nearly died
Because I paused to look at the snowy show
Of common flowers. The young driver saw nothing.
Only the oldest of instincts made me leap
Onto the pollen-dusted bank an instant
Before the car crashed past. In it a white face
Opened, all mouth, but his cry gagged and mute
In mechanical scream. My pale face bloomed red.
I quickly grabbed my humble weeds—and fled.

SOME DAY

Some day when there is no more bread
We will find man has fled
And left the cupboard bare.
            I pray not to be there.

THE NEED

You need to be alone
after dark
with black rock
and blacker sky
if you are going
to clear the world
and sorrow the sea
white as day.

THE MOTH

I caught a moth at the lamp last night,
I felt it flap in my hand,
I took it out to the dark of stars
But it could not understand;

Straight back to the burning lamp it flew,
Beating its wings on the glass,
I took it out to the dark of stars
But it flopped about on the grass ...

I saw the moth by the lamp this dawn
Tattered and dead on the sill,
I took it out to the dark of day —
Where the ants are at it still.

AWARENESS

I have become aware of mortality:
That the stars will hold their fire
And no winds blow across the sea.
I have become aware of infirmity.
While the children's kites fly higher
The autumn's in the leaves for me:
Too well we lived, too swiftly run,
Too deeply loved—our web unspun.

DYINGS

I walked to the end of the harbour
To hear the song of the sea;
But the walls of stone and water
Were mystery to me.

I climbed to the top of the mountain
To grasp the glory of birth;
But the snows of winter had covered
The last corner of earth.

I sprang to the end of the rainbow
To seek the winds running free;
But the width of the years had blinded
The child's vision in me.

THE ST. PAUL'S WEDDING

It was laughable really
this sumptuous service
for a bride and groom
as mortal as the next.
The Royals came like
sparrows to the steps
and took their peacock places
below the dome.

It was very tastefully done of course;
that much we Brits have kept
from our gilt-edged past.

A trumpet sounds the same
whoever hears it blowing
and showy clothes only disguise
so many hungry things.

But it was when the church limped in,
in golden glitter and pomp sublime
(a third world's wealth
in one man's decking out) —
it was then I switched off
the bright sin of television.

I took my shepherd dog
for a walk along the bay,
looked out to a fishing boat
nodding and bobbing.

It was a long way then, as now,
from Galilee to Rome.
Christ lived as a working lad
and went with mere fishermen
to the scaly local.

I wonder where he was
when this couple wed?
He must have seen it on the box.

COMPOSITION IN GREY

A weak winter, cruel in the city street:
Cobbles are broken up, the clay laid bare,
Red lantern lights line lonely pipes and stare
Unwinking testimony of dull, wet weeks:
Weeks of worn, windy, wishy-washy skies,
Of soapy streets and gritty spray-soaked legs,
Laundry lines tossing out the plastic pegs
And bairns in prams with loud, protesting cries.
A period-piece, a composition drawn in grey:
Grey dawn, grey noon, grey curtains to a grimy
                                    greetin day.

A weak winter, cruel in the city street:
Closes are crowded with the children crying,
Or scribbling secret things, or pulling hair,
Mother comes from work—weary up the stair,
Men stand before fires—steaming and swearing,
Telling of dog bets, of unemployment,
The horror film on at the Cross at eight,
The game on the morn, the crowd at the gate,
The stupid gaffer the bosses have sent . . .
In a hundred ends they watch the telly— a
                                    thriller play.
They go to sleep. Grey things grow great and
                        golden in their way.

OF MEN

Out in the night of panther black
Our clawed minds crackle with thoughts,
Unheard, but ready to scream,
Shot through with terrible terrors,
Stalked by the might have been.

So do we enter the jungle then:
Fire-hearted,
    Moist-palmed,
        Naked apes.
But through the rain that rods us,
Stunningly,
In the lightning flash,
We glimpse the majesty of men.

A LARK SINGS

A lark sings for no joy,
No love, no fear,
But as he soars and sings
He sheds no tear.
Would we could go through life so free!
But there's so much of earth in you
  — and me.

STUDY WALLS

A stone dog peers out of a stone door
Telling of love down two thousand years —
Immortalised on a Turkish tomb.
The Taj Mahal, and the Baby Taj, are calm
Man-made temples among the gods of hills:
Nanda Devi, Matterhorn, An Teallach,
Alpamayo, Bietschhorn, Cobbler,
A row of Arctic peaks—a mere sample
Of the scores that pin my soul in view.
There are Berber plates, an old school badge,
A pennant from "Veeps" cycle tours.
Dali's *Christ of St. John of the Cross*
Is largest of all, next a M'Cheyne text
Of fading Victorian colours. *Kitchy* and *Storm*
Look at me from their happy heights.
There are cuttings showing cheery Braehead
Parties on Snowdon or camped east of the Ben,
Bird prints, flower prints, feathers (flamingo, owl)
and whole rows of climbing journals,
the *Cascades d'Ouzzoud* (loveliest of all falls),
Ship loves: *Captain Scott, Eye of the Wind*,
Which have taken me on the chancy seas,
Camp fire scenes, seascapes, sunsets ...
All these are pinned among the junk of work,
A random crowdedness, bewildering others
But this is how my life, danced about earth,
Came bit by bit in happy disarray to stir
The memories by their shadows on my walls.

LENBACH'S *SHEPHERD BOY*

Do you know Lenbach's *Shepherd Boy*?
No great painting
But a postcard print of it
Was once an inspiration
To this boy!
The lad lies on his back
Among the grasses,
Eyes shaded, looking into the sky.
That, then, for me,
Was a picture of life,
Of hope blue as the sky
Under which he sprawls.
This is the sin now:
We adults do not lie back
In scented grasses
Under lark song.
(We are far too busy!)
The lad's feet are bare --
And when did you
Last curl toes in dewy cold
Upon some summer hill?

I pinned that print
Twenty years ago
Onto my study door
But have not looked at it for months.
Tonight I did --
And went out into the dark
To beg forgiveness
Of the starry skies
For my forsaken faith
And the lost confidence
Of youth.

HYPOCRITE

I, who'd swim star fountains,
Let the moon go down.
I, who dream of mountains,
Sleep within a town.

DAYDREAMING

I hear the mountains murmur
In city lanes to cry . . .
    It is the typists' chatter
    Or tramcars trundling by.

I hear it deeper, further,
It is not city noise . . .
    You hear the grey rain blatter,
    The wind-borne cry of boys.

COVENTRY CATHEDRAL

The notice said:
"Service at 5 p.m."
so I walked round the town
and had some tea
and was there for five.

I sat with my thoughts
and mathematical spaces,
book-shelf windows,
grub-bodied Christ—these
were kind distractions to my prayers.
They fulfilled intentions —
led upwards.

But there was no service.
I sat alone.

Eventually there were echoing steps
and hands emptying two coffers
labelled **Give! Give!**

My God —
How He gave!

CITY SUNSET

The quiet setting of the sun rims a song
that echoes from hills (home-flamed hills of long,
bracken slopes and rowan-red woods) to sway
into a heart that for a while would stay.

As I halt in the turmoil of the street
I can hear the singing: small, hidden, sweet;
where the rush of meaningless men go by
the whispering echo of that other sky
returns and, in the grimy, grey-clad eve,
it flames up—like so many forced to leave –
the very soot is silvered as the night
wings its way. Now the heart takes flight!
Ah sun, sing softly on the hills I knew
And in the seeking of this heart, renew, renew.

HOME THOUGHTS FROM SUBURBIA

I can bear my lot of city toil,
Commuting with the rest,
For I've a dream of ending —
An island in the west.

With a *machair* sky out westward
And winds that smell of sea,
There's the urban grace of patience —
Please pass my cup of tea.

FLU

Long, lifeless days of black within,
A clamminess of soul,
When the world is one sore sniffle
And inner self is foul.
How long? how long? The plea seems vain,
But, ah, the casual balm of health again.

WHY

There were curlews over the street
(flamingo-pink in the sunset flush),
there was a titter of stiletto heels
and the male ache of office feet
returning to the council flats.

    And I walked with a briefcase with the rest,
glad for tea and a long evening—wearily
content before a blaze of coal
and driftwood from strange shores;

        But discontent at the stretch of wings,
        the cry of the wild way to the sea.
I could hear the wimping of waves from bed;
and one curlew's curdled cry.

        I cursed the cold content of things;
        and the bird that asked my why.

HILL LOVE

We looked over the white sea
after we'd climbed the brae
Back o Keppoch
The isles were there as always:
abstract shapes abreast the tide
and phallic peaks in Skye.
We looked below us, down
the pulsing autumn slopes
gripped in a randy sun.
A stag roared and roared
and with his harem circled our knock
oblivious of all but lust.
We forgot the abstract, the hills, the view . . .
in the bracken, by starlight,
had found our peace.

WHAT ARE YOU THINKING ABOUT?

We sit by the old tent,
with old scents and sounds
returning with the sun;
sucked from the earth,
watered by melting snow —
it's a dream of long ago.

An ant runs drunk on the groundsheet,
an owl shivers its voice on the afternoon,
a sheep bleats on and on (but distantly),
the river is all fishscales, the sun gold,
and Assynt stony white, and very old.

Through the smoke I see
A thousand sites, and sigh
for the memories. I sigh
so audibly that she
asks a question.
I have to beg her
to repeat her words
for they sped—first swallows—
and passed me by
to star the sky.

WINDOWS

It is the dead eyes,
Dark, as if spectacled
In despair;
Stark squares, yet
Cataracted:
It is these that warn
The seeing eye
From afar
That the house is dead.

It may raise walls
Of warm stone,
Grow in silence
Unfenced,
But the shock is the eyes,
Those dead eyes
Blank from a mile away.

So we approach the howff
In silence,
Push open a hingeless door --
Like a broken nose
Between the black eyes
That turn in
To question the soul.

The glass
Has gone from the windows.

GLEN PEAN COTTAGE

The air thickens
In the deserted glen.
Only the dusk moves.
I sit out
Under ash,
Under a black crag, the hillside red
With day closed, only the faint stirring
Of the dusk wind to remind of time.
The night stars us
With silence,
Broken by the murmurings
Of water —
Prayers in the cathedral hills
Of our schisty hearts.
I sit long
With silence.
I sleep sound, under crossed rafters,
Under moonlight, postponing for ever
If I could
The return south.
Death would be easy in this quiet place.
It was just life that proved intolerable.
My grandfather's grandfather fled it
But I return —
For my single night,
My solitary dusk,
The homeless
Home, at peace
With silence.

THE SHIELING

Late I found it—by the western sea —
Roofless in simplicity.
The London owner would not let me buy
The four grey walls and the roof of sky.

But that was then—today a pile of stone
And nettles covers all my dream of home.

PREFERENCE

I preferred the meadow and the skylark song
With cowslips honey-gold in the tangled grass.
The bungalows have "No such weeds!" - trained gardens
Where sparrows squat in urban squalor.

But wait—bird, seed, flower —man has his day
And his concrete world has its final shock.
Flowers and birds may yet possess an empty world when all
The vanities of man have, seedless, blown beyond recall.

UIG: DEPARTURE PORT

There is no need for sorrow.
Let the gales clear the land.
Let the clouds spill on the braes.
There is no barbed wire
To catch life's white sheet,
Frozen, hard as stone.

There is no need to fear.
A *tigh dubh* is built
To brave every storm
Blowing off the mean Minch.

I shall sleep dreamless
Under the lichened stones,
Under the snows of winter,
Under the summer cottongrass,
My rest forever looking west,
West, over sea and sky,
West, where all dreams lie.

LEWIS

It is a strange land:
grey-shrouded, beaten by gales,
pitted by a merciless faith.

Only a stray geranium
peers through a lace curtain
at the horizontal rain.
It is afraid to be seen, blooming,
on this peat-black Sabbath.

Here are the oldest rocks in the world.
They are a work of coloured joy.
They ambush bays of sand
white as innocence.
But our houses are grey.

An empty bottle bobs on a moor loch,
dipping past a tumbled broch,
shadowed by tall stones,
past rings of destiny —
unfulfilled.

The piping rain reels
down the hollows of the lazy beds,
following the old course
that leads to the sea.

I could sing it better in Gaelic
but our grandchildren will just speak
the alien tongue. We will have gone —
like the steady flight of the solan
round the Butt of the world.

We are a grey people in a grey land;
because grey is the colour of dusk
and dusk takes the loom of the night.

SUNDAY

I hardly noticed the kid really
though I swerved to avoid his wobbly course
along the High Street.
I do remember the red boots
(red wellies)
that pedalled furiously ...
There was fair hair down on an elfish grin.
I was in a hurry to get the Sunday papers.
And my mind was on aunt Vera coming to tea.

Coming back there was a small crowd at the junction;
a mangled bike lay by the fountain
and sticking out from under a fat Volvo
were two red boots, leaning against each other
like children asleep.
The papers (as usual) were full of deaths.
And aunt Vera duly came to tea.

FOR SOME CHILDREN

For some children
Adventure led them down stairs
And into streets
Half-shadowed with fear,
Half-lit by wonder.

For some children
Adventure drove them up streams
And under stars
To mountains of awe,
Sharp hills of surprise.

Children grow up but, in flash and thunder,
The taking of life is reflected in their eyes.

THESE ARE MY CHILDREN

These are my children: children of the mountain crest,
Children of laughter and the shouting of the west,
Children of the dawning and the splashing of the stream,
Children of the snowstorm and the blowing of a dream,
Children lying as I lay once with back against a cairn,
Children with eyes seeing beyond the violet of the Isles,
Children with hearts beating to the history and the pain,
Children with long thoughts and dreams that soar on
                                        eagle miles,
These are my children, children of the sparkling eyes,
Children full of wonder, full of pains and miseries,
These are my children, on my mountain seeking life,
Learning to laugh for goodness, to quietly bear the strife.
In them I see it all again, the unwearying march of time.
When I shall climb no more these children's children will
                                        be mine.

ACHNASHELLACH

Achnashellach is a tweed-scented weave of trees:
Some willows that send catkins stalking spring,
Some alders trying the waters with timid toes,
Some holly, bloodied with holding together ancient crags,
And larches, which have the decency to blush this autumn
At the pressing bulk of the green serge
Of pines,
And spruce.
They patiently clothe the hard quartz and gritty sandstone,
Retailing a soft, green, summertime.

Here forestry actually dresses the naked hills tastefully,
A couturier's touch on the normal Highland casualness.
High above the trees it may be winter ermine now,
With frozen features on grim faces:
Fuar Tholl,
Moruisg,
But, below, lies Golden Valley, slippered in moss,
Sequined with little waters, grown opulent with trees.
Achnashellach is all trees!
A tree wardrobe for the smart hills' wives,
Piling ring on ring, fur on fur,
In priceless abandon. It both shocks
And thrills as this rich firm robes
The bare fleshiness of our prim minds.

FOOTPRINTS

The bare soul will tramp
deep footprints over trackless snow
to feel less alone
in the dead hills' emptiness.

Silly, for a night of wind and thaw
will wipe the saucer of spilled life.
Where we set blue footprints,
tomorrow, is grass.

RESURRECTION

I like to think one day
(if the world lasts)
I will come secretly
to this hill again.

It may take generations
(from dust to seed to bird)
before my littleness finds
in this loved place
the dream peace
that would satisfy
as immortality.

DREAMS

O, some grow old and dream no more
And some still dream by day, lad,
And some put feet upon their dream
And have a song to sing, lad.

For life is short as one long day
And dew it cannot lie, lad,
So sclim the mountain while you may,
The sap is in the green, lad.

The names of friends I see no more,
Who paddled in the burn, lad;
But waters deep with crafty sweep
Have washed away their dreams, lad.

For some grow old and dream no more
But some still dream by day, lad,
And some put feet upon their dreams
And have a song to sing, lad.

DONNERT GANGEREL

I'm just a donnert gangerel
On a by-way through the murk
But I ken the yett that's best, ma bairn,
An its toll I dinna shirk.

It'll tak ye ower some muckle braes
And ower wi snaw an frost
But in the back end o yer days, ma bairn,
Nae guid thing ye'll hae lost.

Aye, there's mony paths tae tempt ye
But only ane is best;
So tak the yin ma bonnie bairn —
Tis a hunner o the rest.

WUND

The gangrel disna girn at wund
Or warsle wi the storm;
He coories doon tae bide a wee —
There's aye the morn's morn.

GOD AN MAN

The warld's nae bad
An God gets by
But, keekin at man,
It's Why? Why? Why?

VIEWPOINT

Life is yin o they affy hills
Wi aye anither tap tae stairt;
A sair pech, aye, but frae the cairn
The warld's *doon* -in its richtsome airt.

OCHILS IN STEEKIT SIMMER

Sun-dreich muirs, far gulshy sea,
Puir kistit burns, an nae braw bree,
Tummelled hames, deid shielin was,
An lang waesome goldie plovies' cas ...
We fit it oot frae tap tae tap
Wabbit an weary--deed! Ready tae drap.

We sclimmed hauf-deid in the drouth an heat,
Like puddocks pechin in scawed auld peat;
We dooked, scuddy-bare, in pools o green,
Then hame by the plantin's midgy screen ...
We kaiked the warld on yon heigh wey,
Aye, birled it brawly--fir ane het day!

It's aye sae deid—an tae clever's nae cleuch!
Fairmer an fisher an stalker in turn
(Whiles climber or gangrel), each bides a wee,
Each ettlin fir whit he canna richt see ...
Each glowers at the ither, nane bides ower his dey —
An the heicht bides falla—tae kinder oor wey.

(to *clever* is to climb; *cleuch* is clever, and Ben
Cleuch is the highest point in the Ochils)

AYE, THERE'S HILLS

Aye, there's hills they say, rise tae the cloods
An peaks the likes o dreams, mun;
But gies the auld an weel-kent bens,
We'll kaik oorselves at hame, mun.

Aye, there's hills they say, wi burns o ice
An unco things an a, mun;
Ye'd better bide wi tweedy braes,
Wir doucer hills o hame, mun.

Aye, there's hills they say tak affy time
Tae sclim richt tae the cairn, mun;
But whaur's the sense in that ava?
I'll hae ma piece at hame, mun.

THE YEARS GANG WHEECH

The years gang wheech—like windy stoor —
Ane month a week, ane day an oor.
Nae secon's lang enough fir me
Whad lifer live than peeley dee.

JOUKIN

Tae thole the gree thet ithers gie
Snae form o douce gentility —
Mair liker it's a wey tae jouk
The clouts o dour reality.

.

THRIFT

Thrift they ca it fir it bides
Dourly by the threshin tides.

Thrift they ca it fir it laps
Coorsest, wae-wan, moontain taps.

The name's a scunner! Sic rash
O fleurs tae cairpit sic trash.

Here'd be Scotlan, if she list —
Bonny fleur frae staney kist.

INDEX OF FIRST LINES

121

123